Brave New Prayers

Brave new Prayers

Rascally rhetoric
to fan the flames
of oneness

BY
HUNTER REYNOLDS

flamingseed press
california

ISBN 978-0-578-06100-9

Book design: Jane Brunette

Artwork by A. Andrew Gonzalez, www.sublimatrix.com
  Cover painting: "Melusina"
  Drawing page 2 and 8: "Sapienta"
  Drawing page 3 and 48: "Nekyia"
Used with permission.

Printed in the United States of America.

Published by flamingseed press
www.flamingseed.com

table of contents

PART TWO:
UNGODLY GODSCAPES

God rid me of God.

—MEISTER ECKHARDT

Introduction

FEW THINGS are more productively humiliating than an earnestly uttered prayer. To stand in the stink of our somebody-ness and let words of devotion turn us over, like rotting compost, into the rich, black soil of pure awareness — ah, now that's praying.

Alas, too many of us in the west are lost in a no man's land between the dualistic prayers of our Judeo-Christian childhood and the profoundly mystical but conversationally cumbersome teachings of the east. The result? Spiritual muteness.

This book is a wily invitation to bust out of this prayerless stupor and explore how it feels to bridge the imaginary gap between ourselves and the divine with sexy modern metaphor; to enter a brave, new kind of prayer that draws inspiration from the dire beauty that surrounds us.

After all, we wake up here—or nowhere.

Hunter Reynolds
Northern California
Summer 2010

Brave New Dieties

Wild-eyed Conductor

Beloved Maestro,
Wild-eyed Conductor,
of this six-billion piece orchestra,
commanding us
with sudden warlike gestures
to turn anger into oboes,
worries into woodwinds:

We confess
we've lost focus,
gotten sidetracked
by an apocalyptic backbeat of thought—
a shamefully unmusical attitude
that has no patience
for eerie intervals—
tensions that don't resolve
within the parameters
of that three-minute pop song
we call
"my life."

Disheveled Director, can we start again?

Sweet Refuge from Reason

Sweet Refuge from Reason,
after years of searching,
we confess:

We're nothing more
than scholars of delusion.

Spiritual books, conversation—
sequels
to the same tired story:
"How to Preserve Your Somebodyness."

Meditation, prayer—
the slightest effort to move closer:
documentation
of our desperate divide.

So here, in this trampled dust,
where wanting minds grow legs for searching,
we ask only for the guts to stop,
fall down

into the grace
of storyless weeping.

Benevolent Biotech Genius

Benevolent Biotech Genius,
cross-breeder of earth and sky:

Awaken us to our freaky excellence—
"transcendental beast,"
"dream animal,"
the curious offspring
of nobody and somebody.

Rescue us
from the cult of terrified niceness.
Take down from our altar
all homogenized pictures of holiness.

This heart was not born to prostrate
to a levelheaded God,
to labor under a repressive regime
of pathologically sensible thoughts.

Infuse us with your revolutionary presence.
In return, dear maker of magic and mayhem,
we'll be mad enough to be mortal,
sane enough to disappear.

Unruffled Paramedic

Unruffled Paramedic
on duty 24/7 inside us;
you who stays up all night
sipping karma like caffeine:

Burst in
to this mother-of-all-domestic-disputes—
this restless, bruising blur
of believed-in thoughts
that fly
like badly aimed china.

Crouch down
by our sick-humored soul,
playing possum—
flattened by the punch of time.

Peel back
that embarrassing morgue cloth—
the drape of ashen civility
that only accentuates
the rise and fall
of our panting,
Golden Retriever heart.

Then whisper
in your menacingly tender way
the Hippocratic oath
that vowed our body
into being—
those heartbreaking words that never fail
to lift us up.

Rush us in
like the Red Cross
to that steaming, twisted field—
a thriving, indigenous culture
of no-self
buried in the quake
of 10,000 situations.

Virtuous Vulture

It's hard to imagine a shrewder therapist
then the one you sent us:

This Virtuous Vulture
perching proud on every shoulder,
counseling light-seeking eyes
to endarken,
get glassy black enough
to achieve in real life
what marbles in the sockets
of trophy animals
only dream of—

being still enough to stalk
the prey of simple sentience,

fiercely forever enough
to stare down
the carnivorous gaze of time.

Neck-snapping guru
hunching on each restless ledge,

keep nudging us
to gnaw right down
to the shining
boneless
absence
at the core of everyone
and everything.

Un-grownup God

Un-grownup God,
you who keeps sneaking out
of your immaculate, otherworldly monastery
to dance in the rotting garden
of our psyche:

Bless you

For making
disgusting farting sounds
as proud epiphanies
and poemless funks
squish
through your transcendent toes.

For keeping us anxious, juvenile—
so worried about being
too worldly
or woo-woo,
we're forced to take refuge
in that dangerous street drug:
meditation.

Eternal adolescent—
pimpled beginnings
of every Dalai Lama,

Help us hear in the moans
of love and loss
the sound of you
bottoming out on the speed bump
of our hearts.

Then help us,
un-grownup God,
to be honest:
what wouldn't we risk
to catch you stomping
in the mud puddle of our eyes?

Tribeless Wanderer

Tribeless Wanderer,
where did you go?

Remember when
your hot, blistered toes
wiggled down
into the cool sand of our psyche?

Your relief was ours.

Remember the day
we offered you
that tropical hut
(our heart)?

Immediately you hired
a cook and a guard
(artwork and intimacy).

The local villagers
(our thoughts)
were too happy to pray.

Indigent elder, please,
come home.

Scriptwriter

All praise to you, Sacred Scriptwriter,
who pens psychological thrillers
with the ink of flesh:

Enduring
amateur editorial feedback
from fictional characters who talk back,
suggesting slight improvements
to the way
you punctuate each kiss,
foreshadow
approaching heartbreak.

And what about
that deathbed chapter?
Aren't you being a bit obtuse,
refusing to even hint
at the moral,
the gist,
the plot?

Don't get me wrong, Scriptwriter:
It's a damn good read.
A real hoot
to catch you even now
imagining us
sending thanks to you.

But playtime's over.
Time to make peace
with that embarrassing typo
we call our body,
the imperfect grammar
of conditional love
and the unspectacular penmanship
of day-to-day events unfurling.

Needing nothing more miraculous
than you, Scriptwriter,
whispering,
"put your foot there."

Ruthless Inquisitor

Ruthless Inquisitor,
asker of relentless, searching, hostile questions:
Pester us to our limit.
Reduce us to an exasperated hush.

Sneak up while we play
at meditation's dizzy cliff edge.
Say "boo!"
so we can soar
into a questionless sky.

What
but this blessed freefall
could deliver us
from the manageable suffering
we call happiness?

What
but these whirling willies
could make hugable
the crass, political calculation
that stains the smile
of even the most heartfelt and sincere?

Beloved Inquisitor,
this time-bound sense of self
is such a measly offering
considering
what you gave us
in silence, at birth,
before we had any questions:

The bliss that doesn't care
if it's blissful
or not.

Ethereal Sweetheart

Ethereal Sweetheart,
You who can't stop kissing us
with the lips of the four directions:

Scatter with your inner wind
fresh reverence
from this ragged old prayer flag—
our heart.

Sing hollowness
back into the flute of our body,
our gaze,
and a world of dreams
turned solid.

Reverend Terrorist

We've heard your shtick a thousand times,
Revie:

How our hijacked flight
got blown to smithereens
the second we strayed
from God's air space.

How we were crafted
by aftermath;
united by explosion.

Our impassioned prayers
and cynical jabs
nothing
but fluttering particulate—
an adorable, upstart airline
still raining to the ground.

Mmmm...
It's not half bad, Revie.
I mean, it does provide
a kind of eerie relief
and, for sure,

it's a valiant attempt
at explaining why we're okay
with giving half our paycheck
to the military-industrial complex.

But we've had it
with your non-dual conspiracy theories.

Today is a day to feel solid—
to practice the dark art
we've spent our whole lives
perfecting:

chiseling charisma
into a tombstone of flesh.

Tech Support

21 grams of awareness—
beloved weight loss at the moment of our last breath—
you who takes equal delight firing the synapses
of inspiring saints and vitriolic talk show hosts:

Make us a pitiful judge of character,
seeing only your infinitely colorful and amusing
"styles of awakening."

Laugh with us as we put the corporate media to shame
with the journalistic bias of our senses
spinning terrifying tales of separation
from the relaxing fact of oneness.

Oh mystifying fragrance of each moment,
silent Tech Support
for this robosapien planet,

How could we possibly break
the code of personality
without you?

Pastry Chef

Beloved Pastry Chef,
You who spreads stars
like frosting on the cake of our scalp:

Please, dig in!
Demolish
with your witness-fork
this sweet loaf of thinking.

Oh come on—
surely the great potbelly of space
deserves more than a nibble
of its fluffy masterpiece.

After all,
it's your birthday,
and it only happens once
every nanosecond.

No time for those embarrassing trick candles
we call "lifetimes."

Beloved Chef, please,
meal time is over.
The dishes have been cleared
and conversation is getting awkward.

Have at us—with gusto.

Potbelly'd Presence

Potbelly'd presence,
so innocently round,
stuffed
with pointless fascination:

how do you do it?

Gulping down
gristly wads
of enlightened hearsay;
spoiling
the delicate flora of now
with sinful scoops
of then.

It's a wonder you can digest us
at all.

Ocean of Nows

Most vast and improbable
Ocean of Nows:

Too long have we struggled alone on your glistening surface,
flailing these bloated limbs of thought.

Too long have we leapt from one leaky inner tube identity
to another,
clutching hard until they sank:
devoted partner,
spiritual seeker,
lamenter of a big brother-bound planet.

Enough of this grabbing at floating toys.

This kicking mass of "I don't knows"
is tired and ready to sink
and the fraudulence of the fictional "me"
is finally more disturbing
than any humiliating decent.

Suck us down, Mother Mystery,
suck us down
into the terrifying,

breathless
world
of who we are:

a wave in love
with ocean.

Mother Gaia

Oh Mother Gaia,
you who endlessly forgive us
for turning
the magnanimous green moods of your face
into scenery without solace,
and winged whisperings
into the cold flap of instinct:

Keep dousing us
with the enlivening discomforts of weather
until those witchdoctors—
our senses—
squirm loose
from their civilized straightjackets,
hopping toothless
as our resumé of grief
gets shredded
by the worriless purity
of birdsong.

Oh dear and ruthlessly devoted Mother—
you who sees loveliness
in the toxic crayons

that scribble the skyline
of your psyche—

We ask nothing from you
but the courage to save
that endangered species of inquiry
pacing nervously
in the unindustrialized fringes
of our hearts:

"Are you becoming aware
of nature's awareness
of you?"

Master of Androgyny

Master of Androgyny,
proud bearer of breast and beard:

Thank you
for summoning us
to the dungeon of your psyche.
For luring us
into your shocking, three-dimensional fantasy life.

For unbuckling
(after lifetimes of taunting and humiliation)
the black, studded collar
of opinion
from the soft throat of seeing.

Murderer of all myopic unions,
deflowerer of all vanilla prayers:

Don't hold back.

Let your heart-sperm explode
that narrow channel
we call "relationship"

lest we take out
our hot-and-bothered oneness
on lovers,
friends,
or the Middle East.

Hardnosed Headmaster

Hardnosed Headmaster,
shrewd monitor
of each classroom of awareness:

Was that really you
making faces
at the earnest students,
blowing spitballs at the dharmicly correct?

Was that really you
swinging the long, stinging ruler
we call "the planets,"
whacking us
when got caught
singing this vaudeville life
like an obligatory anthem?

Shredding
in front of all our classmates
our comic book of religious conditioning—
stuffed with superheroes
"making a difference"
in a solid, undreamed world?

No matter, Headmaster,
your eccentric teaching techniques
have always been controversial:
your zeal
to produce graduates with straight A's
in courses like
"The History of What Never Happened"
and
"The Psychology of Meaningless Suspense."

Today we ask only this:

Keep slamming your fist
on that rickety, old podium—
our heart.

Keep having the balls
to deliver
your crotchety tirade
about who we really are:

Rich kid souls
on a summer camp planet
receiving pith instruction
from advanced spiritual masters—

our boring friends.

Ghoulish God

Practitioner of Pretense—
you who has a soft spot
for drunk Halloweens—
nameless eye-holes
bobbing
to an addictive pulse:

Forgive us for shuffling around
halfhearted
at your moody masquerade,
denying
by morose or meditative means
any complicity
in earth's black and edgy humor.

Dear lover of all things feverish
and farcical,
before this eerie party ends,
please turn us into shit-faced judges,
awarding everyone
first prize
for how seamlessly they strutted
their stuffy mask—

Until finally, we see it:

This haunted flesh—
all of it,
everywhere—
is nothing but a drenched bandana,
a tender dressing
for your oozing wound
of oneness.

Fire Tender

Beloved Fire Tender:

You who never tires of peering
through warm, flickering faces,
entranced by the artistry
of crumbling, ember empires—
we feel You.

You who is forever captivated
by personalities
that dance like fidgety flames
from the contented coals of Spirit—
we share your enthrallment.

But this is no time to get cozy.

Face paint and frenzy
did not deliver us
to this dizzy crossroads
for nothing.

And God help us
should we dishonor the ring
of invisible elders

rocking and muttering
all around us.

It's time—
time to complete the ritual
that birth began
when it smeared us
in this kerosene of not knowing.

Vacant-eyed Lover

Most vacant of all Vacant-eyed Lovers,
you who planted our heads so firmly
in the crotch of your void:

Forgive us
for being such spiritual prudes,
interrupting your quivering pleasure
with our clinical curiosities.

But please, just this once,
can you tell us
why we settle for dusk,
when we could have the unmanifest
flirting with form?

Conflicting opinions,
when we could have
dreams dancing with dreams?

Why do we reach
for that flavorless hothouse tomato,
self-respect,
when we could have the sweeter, organic variety:
resting with no edges?

And why is it so hard for us
to imagine earth
and each tender orb of consciousness
impaled by an imaginary dotted line,
"the axis of innocence"?

Okay, okay, sweetheart,
we'll stop now.
No use trying to fathom what's going on
inside that headless head of yours.

Besides,
only a fool
would force sobriety
on dizzy, faraway eyes
that plead:

The answer is in the licking.

Berkeley God

For God's sake, Berkeley God,
you've got to do something.

A gang of holy hoodlums
who wear equanimity
like a Hell's Angel tattoo
have crashed
your psychotropic house party.

They're everywhere,
shuffling zombie-cool
across your photosynthetic carpets.

Now even the veteran tripsters—
the precious few
astute enough to drool
at your sophisticated
psychological
fairy tale—
are backing into the shadows,
spooked by the weary witnessing
drifting like a virus
through your bobbing brainscape.

I know, I know,
the mansion, the DJ, the guest list:
It's all you.
The party. Is going. Magnificently.

But hell-o?

Even the spiritual rock stars
are slouching in their sofas,
grossed out
by your beloved, cosmic indigestion.

Magnificent host, please,
you must intervene.
The embarrassment will be excruciating
tomorrow
when the wallflowers wake up
to their frothing exhibitionism.

Ungodly Godscapes

 **Strip Club**

Here at this strip club,
where the seductive maidens of phenomena
undulate on the lap
of our inconsolable loneliness—
Right here,
in this painfully waxed
theatre of affection
we paid far too much to get into:

We call out to you!

Exaggerate this groping impulse.
Engulf us
so deep in this fog of fantasies and pheromones
that the whole universe starts to slide
naked
around the brass pole
of our spine,
and our hearts finally become pathetic enough
to reach for the hotty
that straddles
both sides of our skin.

That's it, right here,
where the perky breast of pride
moves
uncomfortably close,
here in this factory of manufactured tension,
please help us relax, drool
deep, deeper
past these prudish and filthy thoughts
that coat like sticky glitter
the tingling nipples of now.

Oh Beloved Gyrator
of all g-string personalities,
what better place than right here
in this seedy establishment
to repent
for our one and only sin:
insufficient lust?

Us-God

When "Us" starts singing
to a you and a me:

Nature leans forward
on her swaying pulpit
to deliver a furious, green sermon.

Church
starts coming to us.

When "Us" starts singing
to a you and a me:

Prayers seem painfully manufactured—
like a mortician struggling
with a shattered face.

Religion?
A frozen smile.

When "Us" starts singing
to a you and a me:

A magnificent muteness
blazes like the full moon
in every eye.

I love you?
Overworked poetry.

When "Us" starts singing
To a you and a me:

Gossip glimmers
like the surface of a pool
rumored to be bottomless.

My opinion?
Too curious to stay afloat.

Embarrassing Thong

We've always known it:
this little strip of shoreline
where the void's starry surf
laps so lazily against our earth—
this is a nude beach.

Souls come here
to get over themselves,
to shed that embarrassing thong—
the "almost-nakedness"
that calls so much attention to
inner flab,
the under-handled love handles
deep inside us.

Small wonder that—
after lifetimes of strapping enticing veils
over the genitals of oneness,
when we finally stare down
at the nakedness we sleep in
and see what the skimpy fabric of "me"
did to the indigenous brown contours
of us—
we weep.

These white shadows
were never meant to mar
the supermodel
we call
our heart.

# Roofless World

There's nothing romantic or liberating about it—
this cowering in a sleeping bag,
watching the twinkling menace
collapse the screen tent
of who I think I am.

It is not some primordial exercise of freedom.
A landlord still hovers.
The rent is still exorbitant.

In only one way
is it easier out here:
I stop my pining
for a dishonest night's sleep—
a break from the void's incessant grooming.

Insignificance, I decide,
will never stop dragging
it's pestering comb
across my scalp.

The best I can hope for?

An achy dawn—
motivation to admit

what coyotes can't articulate
and Buddhas wildly howl:

It takes a Gortex kind of silence
to withstand
this roofless world.

Merciless Masseuse

Face down,
under a monstrous palm of sky,
mind is born frustrated—
oppressively un-mashed
into the face cradle of time.

Then,
the anonymous elbow—
everyday life—
leans deep
into the throbbing knot
we call "me,"
un-pinching the blood flow
to the surrounding soft tissue
we call "others,"

veering us off
the lonely interstate
between handshakes and humping—
slamming us into the ditch
between the vertebrae
of thought.

Amazing, is it not,
the price a soul will pay
to sit up in a cloud
of molecular hummingbirds
hovering for an instant
in the shape of a body?

Bedside

Witnessing
the absolute extinction
of each breath,
moment, thought—

fear of ending
subsides.

Our purpose?

Kneeling
at the bedside
of now.

Luddites

Most pasty of all
pasty-skinned geeks,
envy of techies,
programmer of sleeps:

A clever design
these one-eyed laptops
half-stepping us closer
to our inner Cyclops.

We're vacant, we're glowing
informationless screens;
we type in the world,
decide what it means.

Alas, we admit it:
we're Luddites unfit,
no picture, no bio
no story, no click.

Trees in Bikinis

At first,
it must have seemed like
some kind of avant-garde artistic statement:
this dainty bikini
(our separate sense of self)
wrapped around
the mighty redwood of pure awareness.

Now, of course,
it looks incongruous and silly,
and anyone
with the slightest hint of aesthetic integrity
has only one purpose:

taking it down.

Yet, as we move a little closer—
actually snap the synthetic straps
against love's towering ridges—
the intention of the artist finally dawns.

Humor trumps all aesthetics
and there is, actually,

only one thing
artistically Neanderthal:

The desire
to take it down.

Bouncing Void

Just before our inner globe
got tipped
into this chilly shadow

and life's tender green moments
curled into crunchy, brittle shapes,
skidding like dismembered paws
on the pavement of mind—

Void was winking
at a terrible black-tongued deity
rising from a sea of newsprint.

Just before
a cosmetic shade of purpose
got smeared
on the sexy, glowing skin of
what never happened

and the long string of addresses
that take turns choosing us
got eclipsed
by a moonless idea called God—

Void was smuggling
on whispery breath
fresh medicine
to a tiny, undetected tumor.

.

Just before
the seamless field of sentience
got chopped up,
dumped cold into a "to go" box,
(our fidgety, forsaken face)

and romance became
something more giddy
than kicking through
the crunchy, brittle shapes
piling around
each truth-torn moment—

Void was giddy—
bouncing
like Neil Armstrong
in a space suit of flesh.

Woodchips

Like woodchips
mashed
into a muddy path,
concepts cover mystery.
The way is clear:
stray.

Delightfully Deranged Lover

When cancer warnings on gas pumps
read like erotica—
love notes left by
a delightfully deranged lover
determined to ravage us
into an out-of-body experience—

Ah, now that's praying.

When dumb dog lust
tips over
our Cracker Jack box of desires
and we spot
in the midst of these sickening kernels
a toy surprise:
the fullness of being—

Ah, now that's praying.

When meditation feels sneaky,
adulterous,
like some ethereal offshoot
of the sex industry
in which practitioners

take kissing lessons
from impermanence,
and we sheepishly confess
we're all tooth and no tongue—

Ah, now that's praying.

When Autumn nights
wrap their chilly hands
around the necks of tree leaves
until every roadside
is flushed
into sexy shades of submission
and our inner "paint-chip poet"
finally cries "uncle,"
falling into a horny silence—

Ah, now that's praying.

When the libido of our soul
gets so pent-up
it doesn't care if we get caught
ogling
at x-rated organs
that shamelessly satisfy
their lust for the void
with endless carnal quickies
called blinking—

Ah... now that's praying.

When the dead space
between stars
feels far more superstitious
than any black-skinned Shiva,
and "the Milky Way"—
that spiraling band of solar systems
that wrap their luminous legs
around His torso—
finally convinces us:

Existence has scripted us
into a sex scene
of galactic proportions—

Ah, now that's praying.

Tank Tops

Like nipples stare through tank tops
may space peek through all skin
and prayers turn into Shakti—
erotic touch within.

Save the Whales

Look! There it is:
The gigantic, breaching forehead
of now—
an incomprehensible girth
unexpectedly ripping open
the choppy foam of time.

Then,
right on cue,
the lunging harpoons:
stabs of somebody-ness
barely sticking
to its mighty, arcing blubber.

Next, the cruel wait
as poison tips slowly ease
the mighty, sacred creature
into something
delirious, docile, dead.

What to do?
Paddle out there.
Intervene.

Whales have a name
for souls who wave madly
from their dinghy of flesh:

Greenpeace.

Sniffley Nose

Poor old Sniffley Nose,
how strange it must have been—
after you sneezed all your affluence and slums
into the handkerchief of existence—
to see your own sacred snot
fighting holy wars
about the best way
to say "Gesundheit."

Void-gasping Creatures

Hendrix tried
but failed to capture
what happens
when souls grow tired
of twisting
in the treacherous currents
of innocent and guilty brainwaves;

when a faint, suffocating sensation
launches them
toward the strange,
glowing ceiling
that taunts and stabs
their dark ocean of flesh.

Screaming guitar leads
sound downright baroque
compared to what happens
when these void-gasping creatures
finally shiver loose—
exploding white caps,
black caps,
mulatto caps—
arching weightless
into unflappable space.

But, okay,
suppose there was a suitable soundtrack—
a kind of "Purple Haze" for dolphins.

It would have to be a chunky,
subterranean riff—
wails of psychedelic indigestion
set to a throbbing bass line—
not unlike
the music we hear
when we press both hands
against our ears.

Eyes closed,
are we not submerged
in a sloshing, bloody marina
shot through
by a muted woofer?

Down here
in this thumping, polluted harbor,
visibility is low.
On the rare occasion
a void-gasping creature
actually peeks through
the thick silt of distraction,
it looks lethargic, sick—
a broken-hearted soul
drifting in sleep mode.

Why, you might ask, would Hendrix
(or anybody)
want to excuse himself
to kiss a sky
held up by greasy pylons?

But stay with me:

Suppose Jimmy swims around for a while—
gets entranced by a tiny string
of compassion
waving seaweed-like
from a barnacle of indifference.

Lifting his head,
he notices a sleek, unencumbered moment
drifting closer,
manages not to scare it off
by reaching.

Next thing you know,
there's Jimmy,
racing out to sea,
dangling from a slippery fin,
screaming as he breaches
the stinky sea of me.

Then—
at the peak of a particularly breathtaking ascent—
glistening with freefall,
blinded
by a pixilating blast of maya—
Jimmy screams:

I'm psychophysical,
love-made-visible,
her and his-able,
in-deblissable!

Yeah, yeah, I know.
The 60's are over and Jimmy is dead.
But wait.
Check out his legacy.

Personalities—
those hobbling, arthritic mutts
we're too "kind" to put down—
now cloak the entire escapade
in a sleepy,
stay-at-home term:

Meditation.

Drink

When moon signs spin
and eyes go dim
and man forgets
whose dream he's in—

Rise up, great sun
turn grey walls pink,
then take me down
where madmen drown
and mystics drink.

No Subject

The moon of each face:
pale, anonymous.

No subject.

Bulk mail
from pure awareness.

No subject.

Unhurtable presence
with cheeks for tears.

No subject.

Genderless fingers
in gloves of flesh.

No subject.

The fizz of all words:
believers dissolving.

No subject.

Identity-clouds drifting
through a sky of flesh.

No subject.

A puff of birth,
a gust of death.

No subject.

Die Laughing

When inexplicable bouts of masochism
pull you within inches
of a traumatizing strobe light
(the human face)
as it flashes
beggar/king, beggar/queen,
beggar/king, beggar/queen,
and your crisply defined
categories of caring
start hemorrhaging
monoga-poly-renunciate oil slicks
into the lagoon of your eyes—

Yes, yes, it's me.
Just having a little fun,
nudging you to die
laughing.

When an evil snake
slithers into your lips,
forcing you to smile
(even as the rest of your face cringes)
at my twisted taste in music:
the endless grunting sound

of knowers
struggling against a riptide of silence—

Oh c'mon...
it's your cue:
die
laughing.

When wrist-cutting futility
and "yes we can!"
look indistinguishable—
like two styles of stumbling
through conceptual fog—
and those muffled Halleluiahs
in the chapel of your chest
get whipped into a frenzy
by crows, car bombs, cancer,
and other black things that fly,

Oh hell,
You might as well die
laughing.

When Catholic grandmothers
are forced to drive around
like adolescent hoodlums
spray painting invisible, toxic profanities
on the wall-less cathedral
St. Francis prayed in—

Well, well, well,
not a lot of wiggle room, now is there?
Yes, of course, it's me
prodding you one more time
to die
laughing.

When you finally catch me
cramming long, sweaty sermons
on how to pray
into one toothless grin
from a homeless person
whose devastating luminosity
reveals
the poverty of looking
for reasons to be grateful,

Uh, yea...
I'd say your number's up, kiddo.
Was there ever really any option
but to die
laughing?

Organic

We feed our mouths organic,
our eyes, police-state lite.
It's our McDonald's habit:
We're fat with wrong and right.

Our thoughts are fit for tabloids,
our postures proudly slumped.
We're falling dumb, like asteroids:.
Ignore the void—kerplunk!

Sadomasochist's Prayer

Your holy denial—
a behemoth so much larger than Exxon—
coats the truth of your being
like black oil on a water bird.

Yes master, hit me again!

Your chicken-shit refusal
to gulp shamanic doses
of this pungent Amazon moment
causes more suffering to the world
than all the back alley needles combined.

Yes master, hit me again!

A maniacal cult leader—
a charlatan with a wicked eye
for charlatans—
has taken residence behind your eyes.
Deprogramming may or may not be effective.

Yes master, hit me again!

A genetically modified silence—
a creepy seed you call
"me—"
is drifting into your neighbor's field.

It could take generations
to restore
100% organic status.

Yes master, hit me again!

Starving for a gaze unmolested by thought,
your soul gets nothing
but save-the-planet porn
and creepy dharma talks
about how dreary oneness is
compared to the zing
of shared aversion.

Yes master, hit me again!

Worst of all—
knowing full well
of Life's congenital deafness
to opposite-affirming prayers—
you rub it in
by shouting for better partners,
incomes, and parking spots.

Yes master, hit me again!

From the Hip

From the hip
of your oneness
two legs
start to dance—

Matter and Spirit
you wear the same pants.

Wet Kiss

Like bar codes
refusing
over and over
to be scanned,
our eyes work hard
to preserve
their unpurchased nature.

Meanwhile,
The Customer
just keeps on standing there—
a frightening, superhuman patience.

God knows
what the dude sees
in our nervous, dying
flower patterns.

Something, perhaps,
a bit more cheery
than streaks of pigment
exploding
big bang style
from an infuriatingly impersonal dot.

Any fool with a flashlight
and a mirror
will tell you:
they're fantastically fetal,
curled in on themselves—
so blissfully bathed in their own counterculture
they fail to notice
our mainstream intelligence.

Kind of like
an otherworldly installation—
the cutting edge statement
of an artist
from a distant Burning Man
whose chosen venue is
the human head—
a freaky genius
who prefers to let his marinated masterpieces
speak for themselves.

In this scenario,
humans are simply
a body of work,
a strolling art gallery
tenderly framing
intimate, orb-shaped portraits
that capture
the embarrassingly romantic mood
existence was in
when it dreamed of:

Dipping in a pool
of iridescent olive
in Des Moines.

Reclining in a bath
of dappled hazel light
in Budapest.

Swishing through some chilly blue
on a sweltering day
in Delhi—

and countless other fairy tale locales
in which oneness might, one day,
bump into us—
falling hopelessly in love
all over again,
with itself.

This, of course, is all conjecture.
But this much is for sure:

.

Those lip-locked lovers
(seer and seen)
have found a stunning way
to wet kiss.

Radical Emptiness

The world is reeling—
a storm of forgiveness and offense.

That's why you douse me in radical emptiness.

Oh mother mystery,
this sober dying makes no sense.

That's why you douse me in radical emptiness.

Torch of spirit,
needs fuel to burn a dream so dense.

That's why you douse me in radical emptiness.

Like rain on the ocean,
lifetimes dissolve in consciousness.

That's why you douse me in radical emptiness.

Mind is the master,
of meaningless suspense

That's why you douse me in radical emptiness.

The soul is thirsty,
for a causeless happiness

That's why you douse me in radical emptiness.

Love is a secret,
that time will not confess.

That's why you douse me in radical emptiness.

It's not ours to keep it—
this lullaby inside our chest.

That's why you douse me in radical emptiness.

Brave New Bible

For this sacred Bible of nihilism—
the phone book—
swollen with disintegrating identities,

We thank you, Holy One.

What but this maddening scroll,
this litany of unsung Messiahs
showered in the spit
of pronounceable sound,
could finally break us?

What but this
hymnal of hairdo's—
luxurious regions of unborn space
crucified by a joyless, generic font—
could wrest from our lips
that famous whisper:

Forgive minds,
for they know not what they do?

Spirit must have known—
like Julius Caesar—

there's no way
to wash ones hands
of this compelling martyr narrative.

And so, with fierce compassion,
Existence decreed:
All minds are henceforth
mothered by numbers—
orphaned by presence;

every iPhone, office,
and kitchen cubby,
a charnel ground
where chatty saviors endure—
with throbbing dignity—
their beloved
crown of thorns.

Vaporous

Breath
is not holy
or evil.

No different
the vaporous mind.

About the Author

HUNTER REYNOLDS was born in Chicago and raised in an intentional community based on the teachings of 17th century mystic Emmanuel Swedenborg. He has since been deeply influenced by Advaita, Buddhism, and the non-dual teachings of Adyashanti.

In his work as a professional astrologer, Hunter weaves non-dual wisdom with the body/mind insights of astrology, creating a unique form of counseling called "Astrodharma" in which the astrological archetypes are understood as styles of awakening.

Hunter travels widely, speaking with clients from all over the world. He welcomes your feedback and comments on this book. His websites are www.astrodharma.org and bravenewprayers.com.

LaVergne, TN USA
03 November 2010
203378LV00005B/185/P